# What I Learned From My Parents

About Life and Love,
Winning and Losing,
Living and Dying

Emily Knight

## *Introductory Remarks from the Author:*

Much of what I learned from my parents I did not realize I was learning. I am not even so sure they realized they were teaching it. Sure, they helped me with my homework and gave intentional lessons when I was doing wrong; but most parents do that. My parents taught me so many more things in the way they lived, by the things that made them laugh, and the things that made them cry. My Mom and Dad faced the universal problems of married people with families – money, in-laws, kids, jobs, etc. But, my Mom and Dad also faced cancer. They faced it head-on, in the 1980's when chemotherapy was just beginning to be the accepted treatment and radiation was still in trial status.

I believe I could have learned so much more had I been paying better attention.

I thought I would start this collection of writings about the things I learned through the lives of my parents with an excerpt of <u>365 Days of Thankfulness</u>:

*I am grateful for lessons I learned from my Mom while she was going through cancer in the 1980's. Shortly after her fortieth birthday my Mom was diagnosed with ovarian cancer that spread throughout her internal organs. I hated (and still hate) cancer and what it does to a person's body. But it was powerless against my Mom's spirit. I learned that nothing was more important to her in this life than her family: my Dad, my brother, and myself. I watched her throw up every other weekend from Friday until Sunday because of the chemotherapy. I watched her undergo more than one surgery in attempts to chop off the ugly head of cancer. I am sure there were other painful and horrendous moments that I did not see. But my Mom never stopped being my Mom. When she could, she still came to our ball games and programs. When she couldn't, she made sure that we knew she wanted to. She still oversaw our homework and quizzed us for our tests; just from her bed instead of the kitchen table. My mom told us that she was enduring all of this because she wanted to be there for us until we were raised. God had given her a job to do, and whatever it took, she was not going to let cancer keep her from doing it. Yes, I HATE cancer! But I learned so much from and about my Mom while she was going through it.*

And also:

*I am thankful for the lessons I learned from my Dad while my Mom was going through cancer in the 1980's. What stands out the most right now are the things that he said and did that I thought at the time was what everyone said or did whose spouse had cancer. He went to all of the appointments with my Mom, listened to all the options, and told her that whatever she decided to do, he would stand by her and go through it with her. He did not demand that she do whatever he thought she should; it was her body and her decision. Remember with me that many of the treatments were experimental back then. He sat with her while she told us (my brother and I were teenagers) what the treatments were, when hers would start, and what she would need from us. I mentioned watching her throw up every other weekend with the chemotherapy. Every time, Dad was sitting there with her holding her hand and the bucket. My Dad talked to my brother and me about what was happening to Mom and what we should expect. Of course, many things happened for which we could not prepare. My Dad was (and is) a rock. I learned about loyalty and faithfulness. I learned about love and life.*

It wasn't until I was in college that I began to realize that my parents were very different from the average parents. My friends' parents were great and all, but my parents were unusually tremendous. I honestly wish I had been a more observant listener.

*Table of Contents:*

1. Love
2. Respect
3. Discipline
4. Honesty
5. Authority
6. Patience
7. Forgiveness
8. Understanding
9. Fairness / Equality
10. Sharing
11. Responsibility
12. Finances
13. Arguing
14. Winning
15. Losing
16. My Toolbox
17. Life
18. Living
19. Dying
20. Conclusion

*Love (Mom & Dad):*

My parents, as did most of their generation, put the welfare of their children in the forefront of every decision. When I was brought home from the hospital, I was engulfed in love. I was loved by my Mom, my Dad, my Grandmother, and my Aunt, my Dad's youngest sister who was still living at home at the time.

My parents met at a YMCA dance while my Dad was stationed at Fort Knox. My Mom was from Kentucky; my Dad was not. He was honorably discharged, there was a wedding, and I came along within a year. Thus, the housing situation – my Dad had been living in the barracks and my Mom had been living at home. They stayed with my Dad's mother in Florida until they were able to get a house. Before I turned two, though, they had decided to move to Louisville, where my Mom's family still lived.

There, they stayed with my Mom's parents until they could get on their feet and find a house. Just after I turned two, we moved into the house where my family would spend the next twenty-plus years.

I start with this story not just because it is the beginning of me, but because of the life-lesson my parents repeated numerous times to my brother and me. From the time we were small children, through our teenage and young adult dating years we were told that we were not ready to get married until we were ready to pay for our own roof. They had lived with both sets of families for six months to a year each and they could tell us for certain that one home was not designed for two families. When I was seventeen, the daughter (*who was also seventeen*) of one of my Mom's friends, married and moved into said friend's basement. Every day for the week before the wedding, my Mom reminded my brother and me that this would never be an option for us. The couple in question could have taken the money they were spending on the wedding and make first and last month's rent on an apartment; or they could wait one year and save all their money for a down payment on a house; or any number of other possibilities, but if it were one of us, the basement would definitely not be a possibility. I learned that love is only the beginning of the relationship. In and of itself, love is never enough; it must be built upon. My parents started filling my toolbox from the day I came home from the hospital.

I am sure that you will not be surprised to know that neither of us ever moved back home. I did return to live with my parents twice during my Mom's recurring battles with cancer, but that was different circumstances and will be a different chapter.

*Love (Mom & Dad):*

I will pick up the story then from our regular house in a regular neighborhood in the regular Mid-Western city of Louisville. I never remember meeting anyone that my parents did not already know or at least had met with us. We knew all of our neighbors. My Mom went to the school and met our teachers. We were never left with a strange babysitter. Even later, after my Mom became ill, we stayed with family or our neighbors.

I am trying to paint a picture for you that plainly depicts two children completely surrounded by love. Until I became an adult, I did not realize how hard my parents worked at making sure all of the people who played a major role in our lives loved and valued us.

I never remember being made to feel unwanted or in the way by either my Mom or my Dad. Sure, we were told we were "underfoot" or sent to go play outside; but never like they had wished we were not a part of their lives; that we were a burden or that they would rather have not had us.

Before I begin to sound unrealistic, let me assure you that there were times of disagreements, arguments, even fights, within our walls. That will be a different chapter. What I am trying to convey here is that we were never afraid. I trusted the adults in my life. My parents made sure that the adults close to us were trustworthy before they were let to be close to us. I do not ever remember wondering if my Dad were going to come home tonight, or if either of my parents would not be there when I woke up in the morning. I learned the importance of a safe and secure home life.

*Love (Mom & Dad)*

I remember while I was growing up that my Mom touched us and hugged us often; to the point of embarrassment when we were teenagers. She stroked our hair, touched our arms, and kissed our foreheads. She made us feel that she was glad we were with her and that we belonged to her. She told us every day that she loved us. She told us how important we were to her. My Mom went to every school play, every ball game, and every parent – teacher meeting. My Mom made sure that we knew that whatever was important to us was important to her. She also told us how much our dad loved us. She pointed out to us all of the things he did for us. She made sure that we understood that everything both of them did they did for us. My Mom never allowed us to compare her love with my Dad's love. She made sure we understood that he showed it differently.

I remember that while I was growing up my Dad went to work every day. I remember when I was in elementary school and my brother was a baby that my Dad always had two jobs and sometimes he had three jobs. He did this so that my Mom could stay home with us and be our Mom. He showed us every day that he loved us. I do not remember my Dad ever taking a sick day other than when he had his gall bladder removed and missed a few days. He was the youngest man to ever be promoted to supervisor at the plant where he worked. He was not able to attend all of our school or sporting events; but he made sure we could afford the costumes and uniforms and fees.

From my parents I learned that people love differently. Sometimes if you are not paying attention you may miss just how much someone loves you because you are looking for it in ways that you would show love instead of seeing what they are plainly offering you.

*Respect (Mom):*

My Mom repeatedly taught us that all people deserve equal respect. As all children do, my brother, cousins and I occasionally poked fun at those who were different than us. Children do not instinctively know what to do or how to handle the situation when presented with someone with a deformity, speech impediment, or other glaring difference from what they are used to encountering. My Mom taught us to do our best to put the other person at ease; to put ourselves in their shoes and think how they must feel. My Mom taught us to be kind to everyone, to treat everyone the same.

One of the greatest ways my Mom taught us respect was through her example. I do not remember my Mom ever speaking disrespectfully to anyone, including her mother-in-law. I remember once that, at least from my perspective, a family member had been less than forthcoming with my Mom in a financial dispute. I was a young adult, not still a child; and I was going to call the person out on it. I was angry that my Mom had been disparaged and disrespected; I was going to let them know that whether or not they got away with what they were planning to do, they had already revealed their true self to our family. I was angrily saying out loud all of the things I could not wait to say to them when they answered the phone. With tears in her eyes, Mom put her fingers over the connection to hang up the phone. She helped me to calm down, then asked me if I would ever let anyone, especially my own children if the Lord should ever bless me with them, talk to her the way that I was about to talk to this person. If the answer is yes, then go ahead and say your piece; but know that I will feel much more of a failure having raised a disrespectful daughter than losing any amount of money could ever make me feel. Needless to say, I did not make that call. I doubt that the family member even knows to this day how angry I was on that day.

*Respect (Dad):*

At a very early age my brother and I were taught to say "Yes, Ma'am" "No, Ma'am" and "Yes, Sir" "No, Sir." At the time, it did not seem significant that the sir or ma'am was added as long as we were not disrespectful. That is, it did not seem significant to me; it was extremely significant to my Dad. After a few swats for "forgetting" we almost always remembered.

When I became a teacher, one of my close friends and I had a disagreement over whether it was necessary to add the sir or ma'am. We were discussing a specific student who rarely did. My friend asserted that it was only because I had been raised in the South that I felt it was so important. I asked my Dad about it, who replied that when the sir or ma'am was added, there could be no question as to the attitude of the respondent. A young person could mask a bad attitude through one word or by complying with an action with no words; but it was harder to mask a bad attitude when looking someone in the eye and responding properly. True, all young people may not have as hard a time getting and keeping their attitudes in check as the daughter of my Dad did, but it is still good practice. After all, obedience with a bad attitude is not really obedience; it is just compliance. A young person who does what their parents or teachers wish just to stay out of trouble is not properly developing and maturing into a young adult. They are just getting older.

From my Mom and Dad I learned to give, accept, and expect respect.

*Discipline (Mom)*

"Don't make me come back there!"

"Go ahead and do it again; make your spanking worth it!"

There were other favorite phrases my Mom used; probably similar ones to your own mom. Looking back, I learn two key lessons here. First, every spanking I got from my Mom, I chose to get. I knew what was going to happen. Secondly, my Mom did not want to spank me. She went to great lengths and gave plenty of warnings. My Mom wanted me to be good because I wanted to be good, not just because she made me to be good.

That was when I was little. As a teenager I distinctly remember this one instance of correction from my Mom that I have shared with almost everyone who has ever sat in my classroom. Mom was telling me to finish a chore before I went to a ball game; I do not remember exactly which chore, but it was probably the dishes. I rolled my eyes (*uh-oh!*) **and said** "Whatever!" Now, I knew better. I had been taught better. I just wanted to do what I wanted to do. Before I even finished the word, my mouth was stinging horribly. There was a terribly painful sensation around my cheek. My Mom had never slapped me before; I hadn't even had a spanking in several years. I ran to my room in tears, a little startled at my Mom's reaction. Several minutes later, my Mom came in and sat on my bed. She hugged me and apologized for slapping me. She shared with me that when she was younger she had promised God that she would only spank her children where God had intended. She lost her temper and she was sorry. God had forgiven her, would I? This was certainly an unexpected turn of events. I was not sure what to do or say. I returned her hug. I told her I knew I had deserved it; I was sorry that I had been disrespectful; I should have already finished my chore, there would not have been an issue: she should forgive me. My Mom said that I was right about all of that; I did deserve a spanking, and now that neither of us was angry, I could have it. This was another unexpected turn of events. I protested that I was too old for that; shouldn't she use some other punishment? Her reply was that I was also too old to talk to my mother that way; I was almost an adult and should know better.

So spanking it was – paddle, prayer, and all.  That was my last spanking and the last time I ever rolled my eyes or spoke disrespectfully to either of my parents.

*Discipline (Dad)*

As an adult, I know that my Dad did not want to spank us either. As a child, though, I am not so sure I could have been convinced. His approach to discipline was very different from my Mom's. He told us if he ever saw us doing (insert undesirable behavior) we would get a spanking: there were no other warnings. My Dad observed degrees of discipline. Minor offenses would warrant one swat, with major offenses like lying warranting more. One thing, though, that was similar was that every disciplinary measure I received, I chose. I knew the boundaries and I knew the consequences. Both of my parents were fairly consistent. Also, they both agreed concerning what was acceptable and unacceptable behavior; Mom just gave more warnings. I think mostly that is just a result of the difference between men and women. Dad wanted it to be over with; Mom wanted not to have to spank.

Through a series of inexplicable events, a friend and I received numerous demerits at the small Bible college we were attending. I had not done anything illegal or immoral, just against the rules, and a few of the offenses carried "compounded" demerits. The story itself is rather humorous now, but definitely was not at the time. I had a few other demerits, and now these compounded offenses put me close to the number for expulsion; actually, close enough to warrant a mandatory meeting with the Vice-President of the college. He opened with prayer then said he had a question for me before I started my explanation. He wanted to know what I thought my parents might do if he called and told them how close I was to being expelled. I told him that I did not have to speculate, I knew what my father would do. He would say that if I let myself get that close to the boundary I knew you had set that I really did not want to be there; he would thank you for calling him and he would come and get me tomorrow. The VP said that I seemed pretty sure of that, and did I want him to call my Dad. No, my Mom was sick, probably in the hospital, and I really did not want to worry them; I was sure that I could finish the semester without getting more demerits: he would not have to expel me. I apologized for the trouble I had already caused him and hoped he would realize that most of the offenses were really just a huge misunderstanding. He was impressed with my willingness to own the consequences, listened to my story, and removed most of the "compounded" demerits. I received the minimum possible amount and the VP, a man with a reputation for sternness, swore me to secrecy for twenty years or until he retired.

From my parents I learned to take responsibility for my own actions. I learned the maturity needed to not rely on them to bail me out. From my parents I learned to be an adult.

*(For my friends who may be reading this, I am referring to the time I was stranded in the Chicago Greyhound station. This means that I was in Chicago, overnight, without a pass . . . I promise you, my nineteen-year-old self neither planned nor desired that experience.)*

*Honesty (Mom)*

One time, when I was in First Grade, I lied to my Mom. I told her I had thanked the neighbor who gave me a ride home from school in the rain. But I had not; I had run from the car to the door without a word. After a very short few minutes, I was overcome with guilt. My parents had majored on honesty in their teaching us – lying was never an acceptable option. I ran in the rain to the neighbor's house, thanked them for the ride, came back and asked my Mom to forgive me. I never lied to my parents again. All of my growing up years and through the difficult teen years, I was always honest with my parents. I couldn't bear to hurt them by lying to them. I am not saying I did not get in trouble or do stupid things as a teenager: I did plenty wrong; I am just saying that I was truthful with my parents about every issue.

Around that same time, age five or six, I put a package of Lifesavers in my pocket at Kroger. I had asked my Mom if I could have them, and she had said yes, to put them in the cart; I liked the feel of them in my pocket instead, though. I had intended to put them with the groceries at the register; but I forgot. While we were loading the car, my Mom said she had forgotten all about my Lifesavers and we would lock the groceries in the car and go back and get them. With a pale white face, I said I had forgotten about them, too, and pulled them out of my pocket. My Mom reminded me that she had told me not to put them in my pocket for just that reason and made me take them back to the manager and apologize to him. She would wait in the car. I went to the lady who had rung up our purchases and asked to see the manager. She tried to help me, but I insisted that my Mom told me I had to talk to him. He came, I showed him the Lifesavers, apologized, and returned them. He was a kind man, forgave me, and said I could keep them, that he would pay for them as a reward for my being honest and I shouldn't let it happen again. I thanked him, but said I was sure that my Mom did not want me to have them.

Mom said that when my dad got home from work, I had to relate this story to him and ask him to spank me. Yes, my Mom made me practice this conversation with her while we put the groceries away. And, yes, my Dad did spank me for stealing the Lifesavers. I never stole anything else – not even a pen from the bank before they chained them down.

From my parents I learned the importance of being honest. From my parents I learned that honesty is much more than just not lying. Hiding the truth, or sharing only the favorable details of a story are also dishonest. As an adult I have been accused by my friends on more than one occasion of being too honest or having standards too high in this area. Thank you, I will accept that compliment.

*Authority (Mom and Dad)*

From the time we were very young, it was a rule that if we got a spanking from any adult, we would get another spanking when we got home. Grandparents, aunts, uncles, teachers: it did not matter from whom the first one came or why; the second one was sure to follow. When we became teenagers, the disciplines were different (See "Discipline" for the story of my last spanking.), but the principle remained the same. If we got in trouble at school, we got in trouble at home. If we told our parents first, it was much better than if another adult had to call them about an instance or an issue.

In Junior High I had a teacher who assigned sentences for my bad attitude. Mrs. Overstreet once assigned me twenty-five sentences because "my attitude was showing." When I handed them in with some smart-alec comment, she doubled the assignment. Another remark, the assignment was re-doubled. Before it was over, I had written the sentences *five-hundred* times! Needless to say, my attitude in history class was much improved.

I am thankful that my parents *always* backed my other authorities. When I "whined" about those five-hundred sentences my parents reminded me that they had also been talking to and working with me regarding my attitude. They told me that they had been praying that someone else that I loved and respected would point it out to me so that I could see the importance of correcting it. I am thankful that my parents did not have a meeting with the teacher to complain that she was too hard on me or that I had enough homework already. My mom actually made me number the sentences to make sure that I did not "accidentally" skip any. Only after I became a teacher myself did I realize what a tremendous gift I had been given by parents who always sided with my authorities.

The sentence that changed my life (or at least my attitude), for those who may be wondering was:

*"Obedience to my teachers in small matters now may result in obedience to the Lord in His will for my life later."*

*Authority* (Mom and Dad)

Also in Junior High, I had a teacher that I *thought* was picking on me. To my knowledge, my parents never met with her or with the principal about her. Instead, they taught me what to do or what not to do and to handle the situation myself. I received the same discipline over demerits received from her as over demerits received from my favorite teachers. I eventually learned how to behave in her class without getting in to trouble.

Also in Junior High, I had a teacher who was **actually** picking on me. Stephen, one of my friends since elementary school, and I were the only two students who ever received demerits in her class. And, boy, did we get them: usually more than one a day, and one time she even wrote us up for smiling too much! I told my parents that whatever punishment they wanted to give me would be worth them meeting with this teacher and the principal. Of course, they refused. They gave the same talk they had given about the other one. I protested that this time I was not "whining" that this teacher really did single out the two of us.

One day this teacher sent Stephen and me out of the room. Were we shocked upon entering the hallway to see that standing there was the principal. He had been listening outside the door for the entire class period. He had heard the whole thing. He knew that we were being unjustly treated. He said he would talk to our parents and that we should not say anything to the other students.

My parents never let on that they were going to say anything to the principal, but they were the reason that he was in the hallway during that period. They had said nothing to me, but they were concerned enough to ask the principal to check on it. If I had not been sent to the hallway that day, I may have never known that my parents had done anything about this teacher at all. As a teacher, I have greatly appreciated parents who have approached me privately if their child was struggling with my teaching style. Usually, it only takes a little extra time with the student to help each of you understand one another better.

*Patience (Dad)*

My dad taught me how to ride a bike. He did not use the same kind of patience that my mom did when teaching me other things. He did not use a soft voice or many encouraging words. What he did do, however, was stay out on the street with me, helping me back on each time I fell until I got it right. He ran down the road holding the seat over and over again until I didn't need him to any more.

This is the same patience my Dad used in teaching me about dating. He never disapproved of anyone whom I had introduced to him. He would just ask questions about what I admired about my date, what attracted me to him, what I saw in our future together. When I was finally ready to be engaged, my Dad's final question was "What are you going to do if this one doesn't work out?" I started sobbing uncontrollably, because I had not even considered the rest of my life without this man in it; I knew he was the one. Dad said that was the same answer (without the crying) that the young man had given when he asked permission to propose; would I like for him to say yes?

Dad showed patience by doing whereas Mom showed patience by listening. I am so thankful for the balance that I was privileged to experience by parents who truly wanted what was best for me.

*Patience (Mom)*

My Mom was the best listener! She was always eager to hear about our day at school. She was always full of questions. I have always felt like my mother understood me. I know my brother feels the same way. Mom was always there for us.

She helped us with our spelling words and math facts until we knew them. She never made us feel slow no matter how long it took to master the list. My brother had a speech impediment when he was learning to talk; my Mom worked for hours a day with him until he overcame that. By the time he was old enough to go to school no one even knew that he had had trouble speaking. Mom made up games where we had to say the words he needed help on. The winner always got a special prize. Sometimes, I got to win, too.

When we reached our teen years, Mom would listen tirelessly about the cute new boy in my class, or with equal attention to the drama when he liked my arch-rival instead of me.

Mom showed patience by listening whereas Dad showed patience by doing. I am so thankful for the balance that I was privileged to experience by parents who truly wanted what was best for me.

*Friendship, Mom and Dad*

While I was away at Bible college and my brother was in Christian school, my parents went through a hard situation that involved not only the betrayal of someone in church leadership, but also the disloyalty of a few people they had considered close friends. My brother actually had to change schools for his senior year. His class was the K-4 when our Christian school opened and he had attended there the ensuing thirteen years. This was not a good experience for him. My parents had started attending this church only a few years after they moved to Louisville. They had both been raised in church, but were not faithful as young adults. They had good friends who had helped them grow in the Christian life; friends with whom they were raising their children. Also, remember with me that my Mom was undergoing her cancer treatments during my college and my brother's high school years. They really needed friends at this time.

Sadly, I have learned in years of inviting people to church and working in various outreach ministries, that many people in many different states had been hurt by church leadership in the 70's and 80's. I have met countless people who "used to _____." I have not met many who have a daughter serving on a mission field. Somehow, my parents managed to not dwell on the negatives of what happened. They were thankful for the friends who stayed with them and helped my Mom; they were thankful for what they learned of the Bible and the Christian life; they were thankful for the Sunday-School teachers who had loved their kids.

My parents never spoke of what happened. The only answer I could ever get from my Dad was that the love of money is the root of all evil. They had decided to not speak badly of anyone. My Dad told me that he wanted me to love everybody the same as I had loved them before I went to college; he and Mom did not want to be the ones to take away any of my relationships, or to cause me to be bitter or choose sides. I have a great respect and admiration for the maturity my brother showed in also not relating to me any of the pettiness, smallness, or even meanness he witnessed. His view of and responses to this situation are my brother's story, not mine. My parents were still going to be friends to their friends.

I know that my Dad saw one of the couples who had wronged them stranded with a flat tire. He stopped, changed the tire for them, and bought them a new spare. I know this because I ran into them at a shopping store, they related this story to me, and they told me how surprised they were that my father was so kind to them after what they had done. I simply said, "That's my Dad!" and turned the conversation to their kids before they could tell me what it was they had done.

I never returned to my true "home church" where I had grown up. Eventually, it dissolved. I have seen many of the people in other churches in the area and some of my old friends and my parents' true friends, have found me on Facebook, but I never really knew the horrible circumstances that Satan used to turn so many people away from serving the Lord.

I learned from my parents not just to take the high-road, but *how* to take the high-road.

*Forgiveness (Mom and Dad)*

Of course, the entry on Friendship, could also apply here regarding forgiveness. The most important thing I believe my parents taught us about forgiveness is that true forgiveness does not bring up the fault again. Ever. If it is forgiven, it is forgotten. If a behavior becomes a pattern, it must be dealt with differently. Of course, one should not condone or even tolerate repeated abuse. I am writing here concerning a fault or mistake. My parents truly forgave those who wronged them at church and refused to force their burden of forgiveness or bitterness on their children.

But, also, my parents forgave us. My brother and I both did stupid things when we were teenagers or young adults. My parents forgave us. They did not make that choice define our lives. We did not have to hear about how ignorant, immature, or foolish we had been every time we had a family gathering. They gave us space and time to grow and mature. They talked to us. They made sure we knew they would always be our parents, no matter what. There was nothing we could do that would make them stop loving us. There was nothing we could do that they could not forgive.

As much as humanly possible, I learned about God's forgiveness through my parents' example.

*Understanding (Mom)*

Have I mentioned what a good listener my Mom was? I believe a large part of understanding someone begins with listening to them. Mom always seemed to take my side, regardless of the situation. Even in the instances when I felt the teacher was picking on me, my Mom's responses were classic:

"That must be very upsetting to you."

"How frustrating!"

"I can see why that would bother you."

But, the follow-up questions were just as classic:

"What did you do or say to make that person react like that?"

"How do you think the other person felt at that time?"

"What are you going to do about it?"

Mom did not fix the problem for me or alter the situation. She did, however, help to guide my responses to the people involved in the situation. She allowed me to handle it, even when my choices were not necessarily the best.

When the boy I liked in high-school started dating my "arch-rival" I decided to stop talking to both of them. *(A very mature response, I know.)* Mom told me that then instead of just losing a boyfriend, I would lose two good friends. She did not force me to talk to them, though. And, she was right; I did miss out on two good friendships.

I am thankful that my Mom listened and tried to understand. I have never had a friend who understood me better than my Mom did. I am also grateful for her teaching me to think of the other person in the situation. I have not always done this, but the times that I have, I have been able to respond rather than react to the perceived wrongs. If I had listened to my Mom and the inner voice she gave me I would have had far less conflicts in life's many and various relationships. You see, my Mom not only understood me, but also understood both the other person as well as the situation itself much more than I did. No one else on this earth has ever wanted me to be happy and contented as much as my Mom did. And what is the key to this wonderful insight and understanding, you may be asking? Time. It takes time to listen, time to pray, time to heal, time to help, time to know, time to be known. My Mom understood me so well because she invested so much time with and in me.

*Understanding (Dad)*

More than any other person in my life, my Dad helped me to understand life. Although Jesus may judge our motives, others are mainly concerned with our actions. The teacher wants our homework turned in. The boss wants us to show up and work while we are at work. Our friends want us to be there for them: the once-in-a-lifetime events as well as the daily events. Your family accepts you; your friends that are like family accept you: to everyone else you are an unproven entity. So, prove yourself. Have character. Have fun. Laugh at yourself when you make a mistake. Know when to speak up for yourself and know when to be quiet and let life take its course.

Growing up, I never really felt like my Dad understood me. My Dad did not talk much. The older and wiser I grow, the more I realize why. I am a lot like my Dad; I think he understood me much more than I realized. Almost every time I try to have a heart-to heart discussion with anyone, I am completely misunderstood. Friends, family, boyfriends, students, doesn't really matter the content or purpose; they don't truly understand what I am trying to convey to them. I took to writing so I could have a do-over, a re-edit.

I think my Dad has experienced some of this same frustration. I am not sure, though; he doesn't talk about it much.

I do know, though, that when I have taken the time to really listen to what he is trying to convey that my dad has some pretty wise and sage advice. I wish I would have asked more questions and that I would have really listened to the answers the times I did ask.

*Fairness / Equality (Mom & Dad)*

Neither of my parents was the favorite child growing up. There was a favorite of my grandparents; it just was not either of them. Neither my brother nor I were the favored grandchildren. There was a favorite; it just was not either of us.

My parents told both of us we were the favorite. The favorite boy; the favorite girl; the favorite volley-ball player; the favorite soccer player; etc. ... I carried this philosophy over into my teaching experience. I tried to make every class feel like they were my favorite class. I tried to make every student feel like they were my favorite student.

My Mom and Dad treated us equally, but differently. All of our needs were met; we were always loved and cared about. We were punished the same, but differently. We were punished for the same offenses, but our punishments were not always the same. When we were little, I loved to be alone in my room reading, coloring, playing with my dolls . . . My brother loved to be with my Mom, whatever she was doing. So sending my brother to his room was a punishment; but for me, it was no big deal. When we got older, spankings did not faze my brother, my Mom could not hurt him; but taking away video games was a much bigger deal. I did not care at all about the video games.

At Christmas and Easter, on our birthdays, shopping for school clothes -- each of us had the same amount of money spent on us. On more than one occasion, one or the other of us got change in our Easter basket or Christmas stocking just to make sure everything was even. My parents went to great lengths to make sure not just that we were treated equally, but also that we knew that we were loved equally.

The more I see of unfairness and inequality in the world, the more I appreciate this lesson I learned from my parents.

*Fairness / Equality (Mom & Dad)*

Another important lesson learned about equality was intentionally taught by my parents. We were expected to treat all people with the same respect. We were taught to obey all adults. We were taught to share with everyone. We were taught to be nice to everyone. We were taught not to make fun of others. We were kids; we did not always do this. We made fun of our classmates at times; we were disrespectful at times; but, we were taught better.

I remember one time my Mom heard me making fun of / teasing at one of my classmates. When we got home, she told me why it bothered her so much. Growing up, she was the "fat kid." She got made fun of almost every day. Even the girls she counted as her friends would tease her at the altar of being popular with the "in-crowd." This insight into my Mom's childhood helped me look for the neglected, friendless, unpopular people. Some of my very best and closest lifetime friendships have resulted from me intentionally looking for the person the rest of the crowd was ignoring.

This talk just may have impacted my career as a teacher as well as my service in the bus ministry as much or more than any other single event.

*Sharing (Mom & Dad)*

My family was always willing to share whatever we had with those who needed it. My parents gave rides to my friends, let them stay with us between school and ball games if they lived to far away – and fed them. We often had the single teachers from our Christian school over for supper or a game night. My Dad was always willing to use his truck to help people move.

I believe that much, if not all, of the goodwill I have received as a single teacher for so many years, is a direct result of the way my parents treated our teachers. I am reaping what they sowed. I have had families invite me to meals, pack lunches for me, buy me nice clothes, and any number of other wonderful blessings.

My family gave to our local church. We gave to Missions and the bus Ministry. My Dad spent many, many hours keeping the busses in good repair and running properly. My Dad and some other men from the church built our school gymnasium.

My parents helped our neighbors. My parents helped their families. My parents were unselfish givers and I believe they passed that trait on to my brother and myself. I look for ways to meet the needs of others. I want to share because I have seen the many blessings that my family has reaped because my parents were sharers.

*Responsibility (Dad)*

My brother and I were expected to keep our rooms cleaned, do our chores, go to school, and do our homework. We knew these things were our responsibilities. My parents taught us and trained us to fulfill our responsibilities. Both of us at different times have been described by different bosses as their most valuable employee simply because we showed up on time and did what we were responsible for doing. For one summer I worked the night shift at Wal-Mart, 10pm – 7am. This was not an easy summer for me. At the end of the summer, the project manager offered me the assistant project manager position for the tri-county area simply because I was the only person who showed up every night and actually worked all night.

I realize that my parents are not the only parents who teach the trait of responsibility to their children. Every Christian parent should at least strive to do so. My parents, however, went above and beyond in this area. No excuses were ever tolerated. I remember once throwing up on the way to school. I had said I did not feel well, but I did not have a temperature. After I threw up, I was allowed to come back home after we dropped off my brother. On the rare occasion we did stay home from school due to illness, we stayed in our beds except to eat or use the restroom. We did not camp out on the couch. We most certainly did not go outside after school when our friends got home. We stayed in bed the whole day.

We did our work. We turned in our work on time. Once, when my Mom was having her cancer treatments and Dad was not as diligent about keeping up with our assignments, I decided to choose <u>Gone With the Wind</u> for my book report. My teacher {*Mrs. Brown, for those who know her, or know of her through my other writings*} tried to tell me that it was too long to choose for a report. She did everything to dissuade me short of forbidding it. "I love to read!" I said. "No problem for me," I said. Not wanting to bother my parents at the hospital, my teacher allowed me to attempt this.

Of course, I could not finish such a lengthy novel in the time allotted for a high school book report. I knew I was doomed for a "C" at best because this teacher **always** had as her last question, worth twenty points: "Have you read this book in its entirety? Y or N." Knowing that my teacher had both read the book and seen the movie, I waxed eloquent throughout my report. Not only had I not even finished half of the book, I had also not seen the movie. I made up story lines and even added a few characters, hoping my imaginative creativity might make up for the twenty points taken off for not finishing the book. However, for the first time since seventh grade, the last question had been omitted! The test was over before I realized it was not there. Oh, well, surely she would realize I had no idea what was going on in the actual story when she graded my report.

Almost everyone who has ever written a report has had at least one experience of receiving a "C-" when we fully expected an "A." Can you imagine, though, how I felt when a few days later the reports were handed back and mine had a bright red "A- Nice Job; I didn't think you could do it!" at the top??! But, I hadn't done it ~ I had faked the whole thing. I was expecting a "C." Now, it looked like I had cheated. I hadn't cheated though; I fully intended to answer the last question truthfully. I was even going to include an apology for insisting that I could do it instead of listening to my teacher. After school the next day I went and spoke with my teacher with my prepared apology as well as now a confession. I couldn't keep the "A" but I didn't want an "F." More than that, I did not want to damage the relationship I had developed with this teacher. She believed in me. She listened to me talk often about my Mom's illness. I could not bear the thought of her thinking I had intentionally cheated.

She forgave me. She chose another book for me to read and give another report. She took off points for it being late and in the end I wound up with a "B-." But this story is included here to share with you my Dad's philosophy of responsibility. When things had calmed down from the most recent hospital stay and my teacher was able to discuss this incident with my Dad, he asked her if she would grade the report for <u>Gone With the Wind</u> anyway; he wanted me to finish it. She agreed. Dad made me do that report as well as a paper on Margaret Mitchell (the author). Both were graded by Mrs. Brown. All drafts were considered rough drafts until an "A" was achieved.

This incident evoked a discussion with my dad about what to do when you bite off more than you can chew: close your mouth, smile, and keep chewing. If you commit to something, you see it through. You do not leave a mess for someone else to clean up. You do not shrug it off as unimportant. And also, you learn to think through more possible and likely outcomes before committing to other things in the future.

This lesson came back to me during the homesick days of college, several unpleasant jobs and several unpleasant bosses I have had in my life. It has come back to me when others have gone back on their promises to me. It has come back to me through a few boyfriends and two failed engagements. This lesson has come back to me during the homesick days of my time in Mexico. Through each heartache I have prayed and trusted more. I have learned to fall back on my Heavenly Father as He has proven even more faithful and understanding than my Dad. And,

      I have smiled and kept chewing.

*Finances (Mom & Dad)*

As previously mentioned, my parents lived with both sets of their parents during the beginning years of their marriage. They bought their own home shortly before I turned two. I remember being poor when I was very young. I did not think we were poor at the time, but rather realized it later. We had rice a lot. We had potato soup a lot. We had bologna a lot.

I also remember my Dad being gone a lot when I was little. He worked three jobs so that my Mom could be my Mom. I learned that their children were more important to my parents than money.

When my Dad got a raise at the gas company and could finally quit one of his jobs, my parents decided to take on a school bill instead and enrolled me in the Christian School. The next time he got enough of a raise to quit his weekend job, my Mom started working at the school we attended so that he could also quit his night job. Mom was always home when we were home and the school was close enough to walk; she did not have to stay there all day. I learned that my parents were more important to each other than money.

I cannot remember exactly how old I was when this next story happened, so I am not sure where it fits in the timeline. But, once, I remember this awful smell coming from the kitchen. My parents had fallen susceptible to the credit card ads which were relatively new (at least to the common man) in the seventies. And, as happened to many young couples, I am sure, they had gotten out of control.

What does the awful smell have to do with this? Well, if you are asking, you haven't put it together yet: my Mom was melting their credit cards! Yes, *melting them!* In a pot on the stove, my Mom had put every credit card from her purse and Dad's wallet and they vaporized into a bubbly mess of plastic. (Yes, we threw out that pan.) I learned that my parents thought credit cards were not a good thing.

Much later, as a young adult myself, I fell susceptible to the credit card ads. I should have known better. "I am not my parents, though," I said. "I will exercise better self-control," I said. Of course, I was wrong. My dad, the rock, though? He *helped* me out of the mess without *bailing* me out of it. He took me to his bank where I took out a low-interest loan which he co-signed. He talked to me about finances in general and again about biting off more than I could chew. He told me that although he was sure there wouldn't be any, that Mom was going to keep track of any payments they had to make and that they would come out of my birthday or Christmas presents until they were even. I was so embarrassed at having to have my parents help me in this manner as an adult. No default notices were ever sent to my parents for that loan. I learned that I was more important to my parents than money.

A sort of a footnote to this chapter if you will:

Every time I have moved in my life, my parents have tangibly helped me. My Mom has taken me to the grocery store and filled the refrigerator. My Dad drove me to Arkansas and paid for all of the gas. He also gave me money to move to Mexico. He said he wanted me to have my money for when I got there. I learned that my dreams and ambitions were more important to my parents than money.

*Finances (Mom & Dad)*

On more than one occasion and by more than one friend, my views and practices regarding money have been regarded as "unconventional." I can remember my Dad saying often "It is not anything important. It is just money." Maybe I have carried this sentiment farther than my Dad intended it, or maybe not. But, it is "just money." I have never made a minimum salary a requirement for accepting a job. The only time I remember asking what the salary would be was when I moved to Mexico; I planned to keep my stateside insurance and some other things drafting out of my checking account. Even for "regular" jobs I just prayed whether the Lord would have me to take it or not and left the salary up to Him.

I have refused to "keep score" with friends regarding who owed whom, excepting for road-trips or other pre-planned shares. For the better part of my life I have chosen the "high-road" regarding money and finances. I have never been rich ... a few times I have had more than enough ... a few times my friends have carried me ... a few times I have been very poor ... but never have I been destitute. I firmly and whole-heartedly believe that if I am doing what I sincerely believe what God wants me to do that He will take care of me. I have insurance, I have a plan, I have a salary (most of the time); but if something falls through or a friend is in true need, I am not overly attached to money.

"I have been young and now am old; yet have I not seen the righteous forsaken nor His seed begging bread." ~ Psalm37:25 (KJV)

*Arguing (Mom & Dad)*

I was well into my twenties before I realized that not all adults stop arguing like children. Children say things like "My Dad is stronger," or "Your Mom is ugly," when they are trying to have an argument with another child. Actually, they will say anything they think will hurt the feelings of their opponent whether or not it has anything to do with the game or the toy at the root of the argument. So, too, do immature people bring up various and sundry statements that may or may not be true in order to insult or deeply cut their opponents.

I am grateful that my parents taught us how to handle disagreements. You discuss the pros and cons of the opposing sides, both sides give a little, and usually an agreement can be reached. Statements that do not help to bring forth a resolution should be avoided. Statements that have no relevance to any part of the relationship are just as childish as "Your Mom is ugly."

I am talking about statements like:

"You are exactly like your Father *(or Mother)*."

"You always _____!" / "You never _____!"

"Back in 1972 . . . "

And almost anything that you have to raise your voice in order to point out.


Please do not take this paragraph to say more than it does. I have said things like that numerous times to various people in different relationships and different stages of relationships. But one thing is different from the majority of people who use these statements frequently. I knew I had resorted to them because I had no other recourse. I knew I was wrong. I had looked into my toolbox and realized I did not have anything with which to fix this one. I am not trying to say that I argue perfectly . . . What I am trying to say is that my parents taught me the proper way to have a disagreement. They taught me that sometimes things aren't worth disagreeing over. They taught me that when something is worth arguing over, there is a correct way to handle it. My parents taught me how to lose a disagreement and how to win one graciously.

Some things I have found that I feel about very strongly but have refused to argue about:

1. Various standards regarding music and modesty.
    *(It is usually best to acquiesce to the one that is highest.)*

2. Whether or not angels sing.
    *(I actually have very close friends who think they do not)*

3. What to teach your children about Santa Claus.
    *(I have close friends on both sides of this one; personally, I believe, so I would just be talking, not teaching.)*

4. Whether or not it is right to lie to spare someone's feelings and / or keep from hurting them.

5. Money

Some things I have argued about, but later wish I hadn't:

1. My AT&T bill

2. Obama Care

3. Any presidential election

4. Whose turn it was to wash the dishes

Again, I am sure if you are reading this and you personally know me, you can think of an instance when I have argued over something petty. I am not trying to say I have always followed my parents' advice: I am trying to say that even when I have made mistakes, it was not for lack of teaching. I have gotten angry, I have lost my temper, I have been petulant. But, also, I have apologized. I have owned my wrong. I have gone to the person and asked for forgiveness.

My parents also taught my brother and me how to give and accept apologies. You look the person in the eye, you name for what you are apologizing, say you are sorry, and ask for forgiveness. When you accept an apology, you truly forgive. You do not bring up that instance again. You do not "sit on" their action waiting for the opportune moment to truly hurt them with it later. You forgive.

I have tried to pass this lesson on to every young person who has been under my influence.

*Winning (Mom)*

Winning is what you make it to be.

Winning in life probably has as many definitions as there have been people who ever lived. According to the Scriptures, "success" is defined as not departing from this Book of the Law (*Joshua 1:8*). Following the principles given in the Bible regarding relationships, finances, and ethics is true success.

Mom taught me that winning at the situation was not necessarily always winning. Sometimes we had to operate on a different, often higher, plane. We could win at what we were trying to do while being perceived as the loser by others involved in the situation.

Sometimes we have to give up our own way to have a successful relationship. Sometimes we have to let go of our grip on money or our possessions to be successful financially. Sometimes we have to let go of circumstances or situations we cannot control in order to be successful, or healthy, emotionally. My Mom helped me define many often misunderstood ideas and concepts in our world today. She helped me learn to set my own parameters and make up my own set of definitions. She put so many tools into my toolbox to help me construct and even sometimes shift the foundational paradigms on which my life is being built. My Mom helped me to truly understand the age-old adage: "It's not whether you win or lose but how you play the game."

I am truly grateful to have been given the opportunities and awareness that a change of perspective can grant. To be sure, I have not always availed myself of all of the benefits of this lesson, but I can only blame myself for the times I have lost because of misplaced priorities.

*Winning (Dad)*

Although my Dad imparted the same ideal of winning being your own personal definition, his way of teaching it was drastically different from Mom's. He instilled within us that anything less than our best was a loss. It mattered not what others did or did not do, only whether or not we gave our best.

When I struggled with the multiplication tables in $2^{nd} - 4^{th}$ grades, I wrote them every night until they were memorized. They were not considered memorized until I could beat my Dad with the flash cards.

When I missed a free-throw at a basketball game, I practiced shooting 100 free-throws a night until I had above a 90% average. After that, I missed very few in an actual game.

I was not considered eligible to drive a car just because I passed my driving test and was issued a license to drive from the Commonwealth of Kentucky. I first had to read the owner's manual of the automobile, learn to change a tire as well as check the oil and transmission fluid. I believe this was an effort to help me not feel helpless or stranded in regards to said automobile.

I have a terrible sense of direction. After numerous times of getting lost in my hometown of Louisville, my dad helped me to memorize the streets. The Presidents run East and West, in order, from the river out. The numbers run North and South, with $2^{nd}$ merging into $3^{rd}$ at the end of downtown. Dixie Highway, New Cut Road, and the Outer Loop defined our area of town and I could always get home from these three roads. I still have a terrible sense of direction and have used these mapping memorization "cheats" to help me in the various towns in which I have lived. *(Except in Hot Springs, Arkansas, where there was no "grid" development: I still occasionally got lost there after 16 years.)*

These are just examples of my Dad teaching me to give my best at every task. No excuses, no failure. If I wanted to do it, if I felt God wanted me to do it, I could figure out a way that it could be done.

There are only two tasks that I would have to admit that I truly gave my best and could not at least "pass." One would be singing, or almost anything related to music. I am tone deaf, so that one is fairly self explanatory. I can read music, I took piano lessons, and I did memorize a song on the piano, just to satisfy myself that I truly had given it my best effort.

The other would be cooking. I can prepare enough to keep myself from starving, but anytime I have ever tried to make something for someone else, it has turned into an utter disaster. One time, two of my friends declared a meal I had made was edible and thanked me profusely for the work I had put into it. Every other time, we ended up eating out anyway. My mom was a great cook and tried hard to teach me. Mom and I worked just as hard at my preparing meals as I did at free-throws and the multiplication tables. When my Dad finally declared that I could not master this task, my mom and I were both relieved. We all three agreed that I had truly given it my best effort, and we would just have to be satisfied that scrambled eggs or grilled cheese would be the menu when it was my turn to cook. It was just as hard for Mom to try to teach me something I could not master as it was for the piano teacher who gave up after three lessons. (*Interesting side note: My brother is a fairly decent cook and an A+ griller.*)

However, everything else I have ever tried or felt it was the Lord's will for me to do, I have learned how. I may not have become great at everything, but I at least learned enough to not be a failure. I sometimes wonder just how much could be accomplished in this world if people would just come out of their comfort zones and really try something new.

*My Toolbox*

My parents gave me tools to use throughout my lifetime to help me deal with whatever situations may be presented in my pathway. Just like actual, tangible tools, sometimes they have been forgotten or misplaced; but they are there. Sometimes I have used an upside down screwdriver instead of a hammer; sometimes I have let a problem go, thinking I would get around to it later. At times, I have been so angry that I wanted to throw my tools at the situation (a few times, a person) rather than sit down with the instructions and figure it out. But in each of these situations, the fault lay with the workman: not the manufacturer of the product and definitely not with the tools recommended to utilize with the equipment.

Each chapter heading of this book represents a tool with which my parents provided me. Along the way, I may have had these tools enhanced by a teacher, a pastor, or a friend. Throughout life's journey I may have even added a few tools to my box given to me by others. My parents were not jealous of these tools or the people who gave them to me. They were glad if I had better tools than they did. They would share with me how perhaps their lives may have been better or how they may have made better decisions if they had had the tools or opportunities I was being given. They encouraged me to collect as many tools as possible. My parents sacrificed in order to send me to college so that I could develop a special toolbox just for teachers. They knew I would never be repaid in money all it cost them (and me) to obtain these special tools. However, every student who has ever brought his toolbox to me has benefitted from my parents' sacrifice.

I am grateful for these tools. I am truly sorry for the times in my life when I have misplaced or discarded these tools and lived "good enough" in areas of life which could have been better with a little more effort. I am thankful that my parents gave me the legacy of a complete set of tools for my toolbox. They gave me a better start than either of them enjoyed.

*Life*

" ... For what is your life? It is even a vapour that appeareth for a little time, and then vanisheth away." James 4:14 KJV

Life is so short. I have heard it said that when the days seem long we should remember that the years are short. I think many of us do not fully realize just how much our lives affect the lives of everyone around us. I remember my youth pastor impressing upon us as young people that someday our children would ask us how we faced the decisions of our youth. He wanted us to think about this future conversation with them even as we were in the throes of making the decisions. There are really only two answers to these questions:

"I am glad I did ..." or

"I wish I had ..."

My parents were also constantly encouraging us to think about the future. They wanted us to have the goal of leaving the world better than we found it. My parents' goal for us was that we would enjoy the best possible life that we could. My Dad often told us that he spent his youth digging ditches so that his kids would not have to. My Mom worked hard at giving us a home that we would not want to leave. She wanted us to be mature and ready when it was time to be on our own. She did not want us to be the young people who married too quickly to escape our home life. She did not want us to be the young people who could not wait to turn eighteen and move away. My parents wanted us to have the security and maturity to know that when we were ready, we could achieve whatever it was we had decided to do.

My Mom said often, "Home is where you can go when you cannot go anywhere else." My parents made sure we knew they were always there for us. I like to think they succeeded in their goals: my brother and I pursued our dreams and our goals; we are living happy, productive lives. We love our families and we are passing on the life-lessons we learned from our parents.

*Living*

"Life is made up of all the little things that happen every day while you are waiting and planning for that next big thing." This quote was made famous by Erma Bombeck, I believe, along with: "Normal is just a setting on the dryer."

For my Mom, life was the drawings for the refrigerator, this week's spelling words, volleyball and basketball practices, laundry, Sunday dinners, and countless other little things that come with being a mom: until one day, big news came. News that was so big it would change not only all of our lives, but the lives of so many others around us. The doctor confirmed the diagnosis of cancer. This was the early 1980's; my Mom had just turned forty. The future seemed bleak; not much hope was offered.

My dad told my Mom that whatever she decided to do, he would stand by her and face it with her. He did not want her to go; he did not want to face the teen years of their children alone. He did not want to guilt her into a difficult surgery followed by seemingly endless chemotherapy treatments. They prayed. Mom decided she could not face all it would take to overcome this horrible disease. They would tell the kids together that Mom had only six months to a year to live.

When a family meeting was called, my younger brother and I did not know what to expect. These were rare occurrences in our home. The last time we had had a family meeting was when we had broken the bathroom door – literally broken the hinges from the door frame. We were accusing each other of various imagined causes for this meeting. We were a little scared.

When we had each taken our place in the living room, Dad explained that Mom had been to the doctor and had tests run. She was going to share with us what the doctors had told her. All three of us were looking at Mom; now my brother and I were a lot scared. Years later, Mom told us that at that moment is when she decided to have the surgery and endure the chemotherapy. She looked at us looking at her and knew that we still needed her. She decided to finish rearing her children regardless of the cost.

The anti-nausea treatment had not yet been developed. My Mom was sick from the chemotherapy every other weekend for over two years. I cannot even imagine the pain of the cancer itself. My dad went to every appointment. Sometimes he spent the night with her at the hospital and went to work from there.

One Christmas break my Mom was in the hospital for almost the entire two weeks. My brother and I stayed with my Gramma. Dad told us that our Christmas presents were all under the tree and asked us if we wanted to go home and open them. We just looked at each other. When / How had Mom done all of this shopping? Had Dad done it? Looking back as an adult, with what money were the gifts bought? I still do not know where all of the presents came from that year. My brother and I told Dad that it wasn't really Christmas without all of us being there; we wanted to wait for Mom. Dad left up the lights and the tree and we did wait for my Mom. She came home from the hospital in February; we celebrated Christmas on Valentine's Day that year. My brother got a weight set and I got a clock radio with a timer to set for listening to music before bed. We were all glad to have Mom home.

All of this was going on during my $11^{th}$ grade year through the beginning of my college years; my brother was in $8^{th}$- $11^{th}$ grade. My parents would not hear of me delaying college. They had been looking forward to it as much as I had. Besides, as my Dad put it so eloquently, what would I do? They had done all they could do to prepare me for college. Everything they were going through, they were doing for my brother and me. We should not defeat their purposes.

As I said in my introduction, Mom went right on being our Mom. When she wasn't in the hospital she still oversaw our homework assignments and quizzed us for our tests. Dad rarely signed anything for school without talking it over with Mom. She wanted to still be involved. Her children were her purpose.

My Mom did come through all of the treatments victoriously and was eventually pronounced cancer-free. This was an exciting day for us even though neither of us lived at home at this time. On her eleventh annual wellness checkup, the doctors discovered that the cancer had returned with a vengeance; Mom would win the war this time in a different, more glorious fashion: At the end of her final battle, in 1997, Mom graduated to her Heavenly home.

Mom asked me to come home and stay with her when the cancer returned. She did not want to hire a nurse; she wanted me to take care of her. She knew she was not going to live through it this time. Mom said she was so proud of her children and knew that her job was finished. I took a sabbatical from teaching that year and stayed with my Mom and Dad. She had radiation treatments to manage the pain. They also allowed her to have a morphine drip at her home. You see, Mom insisted that she die at home. She did not want to die in a hospital room or a nursing home. I helped as much as I could, but my Dad bore the brunt of this request. He worked every day; and sat with Mom every night. When she was feeling up to it, he took her out shopping or to dinner. I went with them and helped, but I was not strong enough to get Mom in and out of her wheelchair to take her places by myself. We could only go places when Dad was at work if Mom were strong enough to walk to and from the car.

It was a hard year; however, I am so thankful to have had this time with my parents. I learned much from them during this most trying time of their lives. This time spent with them as an adult is the time I realized just how much I had been given by them. I began to realize just how enriched my life was because of their suffering and sacrifices. This was the year that I began to truly appreciate my parents.

*Dying*

I imagine it is difficult to watch anyone die; especially someone you love. It was extremely difficult for me to watch my Mom die. For several months I tearfully prayed God would let her live. After a while of seeing her suffer and realizing just how much she was hurting, I tearfully began to pray for God's mercy to take her to Heaven.

A few things Mom talked to me about, knowing she was about to die have stayed with me throughout my life. One day she shared with me things she regretted. One was that she and Dad had not found another church, especially after they had moved a little North of Louisville and could have had a fresh start. Another was her regret that I had not married before her passing. She and Dad really loved the man I had last dated; would I not reconsider?

Honestly, I had expected the first regret. She was about to meet the Lord and was probably thinking about the influence and testimony she may have had. But, how could she have a regret for my decisions? This did not seem fair! Truthfully, I really loved the last man I had dated and had been reconsidering. I could not tell Mom this for fear she would call him and have him come down at once. Ours was a quite complicated and multi-faceted relationship. Ours was a quite complicated and multi-faceted break-up. Ours was a truly mutual break up – we had chosen different paths for our lives and this brief time seemed the only time they would intersect on the same plane. Mom patiently listened as I re-explained all of this to her for at least the hundredth time. For at least the hundredth time when I finished, Mom simply and flatly replied that I just did not understand how strong a force true love could be. We could have been happy with each other and she hoped I would realize so before it was too late. This was very hard to hear knowing it would be the last word on the subject I would ever hear from her. I did call him on the day Mom died, because she asked my Dad to let me be the one to tell him. That was the last time I ever talked to him.

Another important thing Mom talked about before her death was the future of our family. It was her desire that we stay close to each other and our Dad and to remember it was our job to take care of each other.

One thing she expressly wanted was for my brother and me to "allow" my Dad to date and remarry. She reminded us of all the boyfriends / girlfriends we had each brought home and how she and Dad had always respected and welcomed them. She did expect, and he had a right to expect, the same from us. She would be in Heaven; she would not be jealous. Mom explained that Dad was young and that if he decided after a while to remarry that would just confirm how important and needful she was to him: not that anyone else could ever take her place, but that someone could fill the terrible void. She explained that if it were the other way around, she would not wish to face the rest of her life alone and that we should not wish such loneliness for Dad. She wished that we would love and accept her, but even if he were to choose "someone young enough to be his daughter" we could at least be nice to her at Christmas. Of course, during this conversation, we were both protesting the fact that she was even talking about a time that she would not be with us. She may have said more, but I am not sure we heard or understood all of her wisdom.

My Dad did remarry a few years after my Mom's death. Although it seems it is always hard to see either of your parents with anyone else, I feel this transition was made so much easier for us because my Mom tried to prepare us for it. I am glad that my Dad is happy. I am thankful that his wife does not feel jealous if we talk about our Mom and special memories at holidays. I am so thankful that my Mom tried to think of what would be best for us instead of only what would be easiest for her.

*Dying, all of us*

The question has often been posed to me whether I think it easier to lose a loved one suddenly or gradually. My learned response has become that it is never easy to lose a loved one. To be sure, I am thankful that my family had the opportunity to say goodbye and to tell my Mom that we loved her. I believe, though, with all of my heart that she already knew this. I am thankful that I was given one more opportunity to hear my Mom tell me what she thought were the most important things for me to learn from her. I am thankful that of all the families in the world I could have been born into, that God chose this one for me. I am thankful for the strength and stability of my Dad and that he remained the same rock no matter what was going on around us.

However, I am not glad for even one minute of pain or suffering that we had to helplessly watch my Mom endure. I am not glad that my brother did not really have the same Mom through his high school years that I did. I am not glad that my niece and nephew did not get to meet their wonderful "Nana." I am not glad that I can no longer talk over my big decisions with my Mom. I am not glad for the hole that has been left in our hearts.

I know that God is all-good, all-wise, and all-knowing. I know that everything that He has chosen is what is best for all of us. That does not mean the path is easy, or even that I always enjoy the scenery. However, I am thankful for the example of trust and strength that I have been privileged to watch. I am thankful for the thousands of ways my life is better because of the choices that were made by Him for me.

*Conclusion:*

I am so grateful for all that I have been given. I am so grateful for my parents and all that they sacrificed to make my life better and richer than it otherwise may have been. Perhaps your parents have done the same for you; or perhaps not. Years ago, when asked in a job interview to rate his relationship with his father, my brother gave what I consider a tremendous response to a question of this nature, regardless of the circumstances, especially if being asked by a stranger:

"Whether or not I rear my children with the same guidelines and principles of faith that our parents did is immaterial. I hope to do for my children exactly what my dad did for me: my very best."

You see, I am writing this book not just for the purpose of honoring my parents, but to encourage the parents of future generations to actually parent their children: to have a purpose in their decisions, to furnish their children with the very best possible tools available. My parents were not perfect. Even though they determined not to argue in front of us, we did sometimes know of their disagreements. They tried to keep it from us, but we knew when there were financial struggles. The point is that throughout every phase of life, my parents did what they believed was best for their children. Perhaps they were wrong occasionally; but not on purpose.

I am thankful for my toolbox and the tools that have been placed there. I am thankful for every parent that has ever chosen (or will choose) me to sharpen and polish the tools of their children by placing them in my classroom. May our generation strive to leave the world better and to better people.

**Epilogue**

*The Most Important Decision*

I would like to personally thank you for taking the time to read my thoughts regarding my parents. If, however, you have never entered into a personal relationship with the Heavenly Father, through His Son, Jesus Christ; and / or are unsure of an eternal home forever with Him in Heaven, please continue reading the Scripture selections included below:

1. We do not deserve Heaven: *"For all have sinned and come short of the glory of God." – Romans 3:23.* At one time or another we have all chosen to disobey God.
2. Our sin has a penalty: *"For the wages {payment} of sin is death; but the gift of God is eternal life through Jesus Christ our Lord." – Romans 6:23.* The payment for our disobedience is Spiritual death and Hell. (Matthew 25:46, Revelation 21:8)
3. Jesus paid our penalty: *"But God commendeth {proved} his love toward us, in that, while we were yet sinners, Christ died for us." – Romans 5:8.* God proved His love for us by giving His only Son to die on the cross for our sin. Jesus rose again the third day {Easter}, conquering death and Hell, and paying our penalty for sin.
4. We must believe on Jesus and accept His payment for our sin: *"That if thou shalt confess with thy mouth the Lord Jesus, and shalt believe in thine heart that God hath raised Him from the dead, thou shalt be saved." – Romans 10:9.* To believe on Jesus Christ as Saviour means to have faith that He died for you, paid the price for your sin, and is **the only** way to Heaven. You can express your belief on Jesus through prayer, but it is the faith and belief that assures you of His acceptance. There are no "magic words."
5. Pray sincerely after this example: "Dear Jesus, I know that I am a sinner and do not deserve Heaven. I believe that You died on the cross, paid the penalty for my sin, and rose again after three days. I am placing my faith and trust in You alone to forgive my sin and take me to Heaven when I die. Thank you for Your gift of eternal life! In Jesus' name, Amen."

Again, thank you for taking the time to read my thoughts. If you have made any decisions as a result of this writing I would sincerely love to know about them. If you have any specific questions or concerns with which I could help you, or prayer requests to share, I would certainly appreciate the opportunity to be a blessing. I can best be contacted by e-mail through my company: *superiorscholasticskills@gmail.com.*

Made in the USA
Columbia, SC
22 November 2020